Samuel Putnam Avery

Samuel P. Avery's Collection of Paintings, by Celebrated Foreign Artists

Samuel Putnam Avery

Samuel P. Avery's Collection of Paintings, by Celebrated Foreign Artists

ISBN/EAN: 9783744617956

Printed in Europe, USA, Canada, Australia, Japan

Cover: Foto ©Thomas Meinert / pixelio.de

More available books at **www.hansebooks.com**

CATALOGUE

OF

SAMUEL P. AVERY'S

COLLECTION

OF

PAINTINGS,

BY CELEBRATED

FOREIGN ARTISTS.

—

*Now on FREE EXHIBITION, day and Evening,
at the*

SOMERVILLE ART GALLERY,

82 Fifth Avenue, cor. of 14th St.

UNTIL SOLD AT AUCTION

ON TUESDAY AND WEDNESDAY EVENINGS, APRIL
23d and 24th.   Beginning at a quarter to eight each evening.

———

R. SOMERVILLE, AUCTIONEER.

———

1872.

CARD.

Samuel P. Avery respectfully announces that he reluctantly offers, at public sale, his valuable stock of Paintings by foreign artists. Delayed by various causes, they arrived late in the season, the large number and size of many of them rendered it impossible to expose them in his small rooms, thus only a portion have been shown. To properly exhibit them, and to accommodate collectors from other cities ; also, to meet the expressed wishes of many persons who prefer to purchase at auction, they are hereby offered in that manner.

This varied and interesting collection was only gathered by assiduous search, during a visit of seven months at the art centers of Europe. The great majority of them were purchased directly from the artists, and a large proportion were painted expressly to my order, on commission, given immediately after the fall of the "Commune," since which time, prices have materially advanced.

A peculiar feature of this collection, is the number of works by young and rising artists, new to this market.

As an illustration of the advantage to buyers in making such selec tions, I would state that during the past five years I sold to the late Mr. Alex. White, twenty-three of the paintings disposed of in his recent sale, and on which an average advance of over one hundred per cent. was realized.

These works are presented in perfect order, in new frames of artistic and varied designs; they will be sold in that good faith which has on all former occasions gained the confidence of the public. Should there be any reservation, it will be expressly stated at the time of sale.

Mr. Rossell has been engaged to deliver the purchases, free of charge.

LIST OF ARTISTS

Represented in the collection of S. P. AVERY, on exhibition at the Somerville Art Gallery, on and after Tuesday, April 16th, 1872.

ALBOY-REBOVET,	DONBAUD,	MOORMANS,
ACCARD,	DESCOFFE,	OMEGANCK,
AUFRAY,	ESCOSURA,	PLASSAN,
ANDERSON,	ESBENS,	PIOT,
BOUGUEREAU,	FRERE (T.),	PREYER,
BOULANGER,	FAUVELET,	RIEFSTAHL,
BRILLOUIN,	GIDE,	ROZZIEWSKI,
BOUGHTON,	GUBB,	ROBINSON,
BAUGNIET,	GLAIZE,	RUDAUX,
BERANGER,	GYSELINCH,	RIZZO,
BRACHO,	HUBLIN,	RIBBE,
BAKALOWICZ,	HAAG,	STROBBEL,
BOURGOIN,	HADAMARD,	SCHELPHOUT.
BOUCHARD,	HUBNER (J.),	SERIG,
BECKER,	JACOBS,	SUS (G.),
COOMANS,	JOURDAN,	SAUVAGE.
COROT,	KAMERER,	SIMPSON,
CABAUD,	KOEKKOEK,	SEIDEL,
CASTRES,	KOLLER,	TISSOT,
CHAVET,	LANDELLE,	TOULMOUCHE,
COMTE,	LEAREL,	THIOLLET,
DELAROCHE,	LEFEVRE,	ULYSSE.
DUVERGER,	LENOIR,	VERBOECHOVEN,
DETAILLE,	LADDELL,	VOLTZ,
DELORT,	LOVEUX,	VAN SCHENDLE,
DARGENT,	LEVENDECHER,	VIBERT,
DENOTER,	MERLE,	WILLEMS,
DIETRICH,	MULLER,	WYANDGAERDT
DELFOSSE,	MRYER, OF BREMEN,	ZAMACOIS.
DIEFFENBACH,		

First Evening's Sale.

TUESDAY, APRIL 23.

BOUCHARD (PIERRE-LOUIS),

Of Lyons. Pupil of Flandrin.

1 Burning Brush. *Edmunds*

GYSELINCKX,

Of Brussels.

2 The Faithful Watcher.

HAAG (JEAN),

Of Elbeuf. Pupil of Dansaert.

3 Washing Dolly's Clothes.
4 Preparing for Dinner.

WYANGAERDT,

Of the Hague.

5 Landscape, Morning.
6   "   Evening

100 VAN SCHENDEL (PIERRE),

Of Brussels, deceased. Pupil of Academy at Antwerp.
Medals 1844, '47; Grand Medals at Brussels and Man-
chester, 1847, '49.

7 Street Scene, Study for Picture.

OMMEGANCK (B. PAUL),

Of Antwerp, deceased.

8 Sheep.

SAUVAGE (PHILLIPI),

Of Villers-le-bel. Pupil of Dupuis and Dansaert.

9 Feeding Chickens.

6

ANDERSON (W.),

Of London.

10 Waiting for a Customer.

FRERE (CHAS. THÉODORE),

Of Paris.   Pupil of Cogniet and Roqueplan.   Medals, 1848, '65.

11 Caravan Approaching Cairo.

THIOLLET (ALEXANDRE),

Of Paris.   Pupil of Drolling and R. Fleury.

12 Sea-shore.

SIMPSON (W. P.),

2 5 0   Of London.

13 " The Monarch of the Glen."

(Enamel painting after Landseer.)

ALBOY-REBOUET (ALFRED-MARIE),

Of Paris.   Pupil of Gleÿre and Gerome.

14 The Piece of Music.   *Edwards*

ESBENS (ETIENNE-EMILE),

Of Bordeaux.   Pupil of Gerome.

15 A Present from the Country.

SIERIG,

Of the Hague.

16 " On the Fence."

BROWN (J. LEWIS),

Of Bordeaux.   Medals, 1865, '66, '67.

17 Prussian Scout.

COROT (JEAN-BAPTISTE),

Of Paris.   Pupil of V. Bertin.   Medals, 1833, 1848, 1855.
1867.   Decorated, 1846, 1857.

18 Landscape, Afternoon.

SUS (GUSTAV),

Siv   Of Dusseldorf.

19 The First Fright.
20 The First Bath.

SEIDEL (C. FREDERICH),
Of Dresden.

21 Flowers.

ROSZEZEWSKI (HENRY-DOMINIQUE),
Of Chezal Benoist.

22 Objects of Art.

ROCK CRYSTAL GOBLET. Perfume Cup, with cover of agate and gold enamelled. Belonged to Catherine de Medicis, carved-wood case; Flemish work, 16th century (from Louvre coll.) Gold enamelled Watch-holder, plain silk, embroidered with silver, furniture of ebony (Museum of Cluny).

CASTRES (EDOUARD),
Of Geneva. Pupil of Zamacois.

23 Man at Arms.

CARAUD (JOSEPH),
Of Cluny. Pupil of Pujol and Muller. Medals, 1859, '61, '63. Legion of Honor, '67.

24 Listening to the Watch.

COOMANS (JOSEPH),

3 ⁓   Of Brussels.

25 Looking out to Sea.

(A Pompeian Lady.)

DARGENT (TAN),

Of Finistére.

26 The Little Sentinel.

MULLER (C. L.),

Of Paris. Pupil of Gros and Cogniet. Medals, 1838, '46, '48, '49, '55, '59. Legion of Honor, 1859. Institute of France, 1864.

27 Female Head.

LESREL (ADOLPHE-ALEXANDRE),

Of Genets. Pupil of Gerome.

28 In the Studio—Model Resting.

STROEBEL (J.),

Of the Hague.

29 Interior.

RUDAUX (EDMOND-ADOLPHE),

Of Verdun.   Pupil of Boulanger and Lavielle.

30 Angling.

DE NOTER (DAVID),
Of Brussels.

31 Fruit, &c.

BRION (GUSTAV),

Of Rothau.   Pupil of Guérin.   Medals, 1853, '59, '61, '63,
'67.   Legion of Honor, 1863.   Medal of Honor, 1868.

32 Fallen Asleep.

BOUGHTON (GEO. II.),
Of Albany,

33 "Put your trust in Providence, and keep your powder dry."

BRILLOUIN (LOUIS-GEO.),

Of St. Jean d'Angely.   Pupil of Drolling and Cabat.
Medals, 1865, '69.   Legion of Honor, 1870.

34 On the Terrace.

3294.50

DELFOSSE (ERNEST),

6 00

Of Antwerp. Pupil of De Keyser.

160. 35 The Declaration.

LEYENDECHER (PAUL),

150

Of Paris. Pupil of Gerome.

100 36 Ruins of St. Cloud.

500 **CHAVET (VICTOR-JOSEPH),**

Of Aix. Pupil of Revoil and Roqueplan. Medals, 1853,
'55, '57. Legion of Honor, 1859.

90. 37 Reading.

HUBNER (JULIUS),

15

Of Dusseldorf. Pupil of his father.

350 38 The Forgotten Word.

HUBNER (JULIUS),

75

Of Dusseldorf. Pupil of his father.

82 50 39 The Dead Bird.

12

ESBENS (ETIENNE-EMILE),

Of Bordeaux. Pupil of Gerome.

4077.   150

275. 40 The Frugal Meal.

DUVERGER (THEO. EMANUEL),

Of Bordeaux. Medals, 1861, '63, '65,

100

260 41 Trying the Weed.

DIETRICH (ADELREID),

Of Dresden.

400

310 42 Study of Wild Flowers.

LOYEUX (CHARLES),

Of Paris. Pupil of Delaroche.

800

230 43 The Duett.

AUFRAY (JOSEPH A.),

Of Paris. Pupil of Barrias.

750

175 44 Maternal Love.

13

5327.00

5327.00

ESBENS (ETIENNE-EMILE),

500   Of Bordeaux.   Pupil of Gerome.

100.   45 The Bracelet.   *1111*

HUBLIN (EMILE-AUGUSTE),

400   Of Angiers.   Pupil of Picot.

265.   46 The Favorite Chicken, Salon of '67.

Cha. Smith 25 11 117

GIDE (THEOPHILE),

Of Paris.   Pupil of Delaroche and Cogniet.   Medals,
200   1861, '65, '66.   Legion of Honor, 1866.

400.   47 Le Sueur submitting his designs to
illustrate the life of St. Bruno, to
the Monks of Chatreux.

LANDELLE (CHARLES),

500   Of Laval.   Pupil of Delaroche.   Medals, 1842, '45, '48,
'55.   Legion of Honor, 1855.

125.   48 Head of a Bacchante,

J. A. C. Gray 115 5 er

14

6217

LESREL (ADOLPHE-ALEXANDRE),

Of Genets. Pupil of Gerome.

300. 49 Petrarch's first meeting with Laura.

BOURGOIN (ADOLPHE),

Of Paris. Pupil of Delaroche and Cogniet. Salon, '70.

495. 50 Selling her Jewels.

ACCARD (EUGENE),

Of Bordeaux. Pupil of Pujol.

200 51 After the game, and no malice.
Salon of 1870.

BOUCHARD (PIERRE-LOUIS),

Of Lyons. Pupil of Flandrin.

140. 52 Italian Girl at Fountain. al on, '70.

ULYSSE (JEAN-JUDE),

Of Blois. Pupil of Chavet, deceased.

500 53 On the Ramparts---Soldier of the
XVIth Century.

7852.00

78 52.00

VERBOECKHOVEN (EUGENE),

Of Brussels. Medals, 1824, '41, '45. Legion of Honor, 1855.

825. 54 Landscape and Cattle, Evening. *7. Plurigee 19 E 94*

750 DESGOFFE (BLAISE),

Of Paris. Pupil of Flandrin. Medals, 1861, '63, '65.

810 55 Bouquet, Rock Crystal Goblet from Kensington Museum.

LEYENDECHER (PAUL),

500 Of Paris. Pupil of Gerome.

260 56 The Palm House.

200 BERANGER (JEAN-BAPTISTE),

Of Serres. Pupil of P. Delaroche. Medals, 1846, '48.

250 57 The Young Mother. *Oehme H N Smith*

800 BOULANGER (GUSTAV-RUDOLPHE),

Of Paris. Pupil of Delaroche and Jollivet. Prize of Rome, 1849. Medals, 1857, '59, '63. Legion of Honor, 1865.

110 58 The Rendezvouz. *Mr. E. Blair*

9.607

ALBOY-REBOUET (ALFRED),

Of Paris. Pupil of Gleyre and Gerome.

150. 59 The Ruined Chateau.

ESCOSURA (IGNACE DE LEON V.),

Of Spain. Pupil of Gerome. Commander of the Order
of Isabella of Spain. Chevalier of the Order of
Charles III, of Spain, and Chevalier of the Order of
Christ, of Portugal.

330 60 Saluting the Portrait.

TISSOT (JAMES),

Of Nantes. Pupil of Flandrin and Lamothe. Medal,
1866.

610 61 The Prelude to the Duel.

DELORT (CHARLES-EDOUARD),

Of Nimes. Pupil of Gleyre and Gerome.

180 62 Pages throwing Dice---Costume end
of XVth Century.

17

10.877, rv

750   CARAUD (JOSEPH),

Of Cluny. Pupil of Pujol and Muller. Medals, 1859,
'61, '63. Legion of Honor, '67.

235 63 Refreshment. *Snedecor*

COOMANS (JOSEPH),

1 200   Of Brussels.

430 64 The Envied Jewels---Pompeian Interior. *Wod, Bradbury,*
S Bonny Green

1 200   RUDAUX (EDMOND-ADOLPHE),

Of Verdun. Pupil of Boulanger and Lavielle.

330 65 Hunters' Rest. *Lament*

3 000   BAUGNIET (CHARLES),

Of Brussels. Pupil of Paelinck and Willems. Chevalier
of the Orders of Leopold of Belgium and Isabella of
Spain.

710 66 The Toilet---Finishing Touch.

18

2582

MERLE (HUGES),

Of St. Marcelin. Pupil of Cogniet. Medals, 1861, 1863.
Legion of Honor, 1866.

67 " Medea."

LENOIR (PAUL-MARIE),

Of Paris. Pupil of Gerome and Jalabert.

68 The Rendezvouz---Persia.

PREYER (PAUL),

Of Dusseldorf. Pupil of his father, A. W. Preyer.

69 Interior.

(*The Fruit, &c., painted by his father.*)

GIDE (THEOPHILE),

Of Paris. Pupil of Delaroche and Cogniet. Medals,
1861, '65, '66. Legion of Honor, 1866.

70 Singing Dervishes at Scutari. Salon,
'70.

19

13977.00

WHITTREDGE (W.)

325. 70*a* Platte River---Colorado.

HART (JAS. M.)

350 70*b* Foggy Morning---Adirondacks.

BAKALOWICZ (LADISLAS),
Of Cracovie, Austria. Pupil of the Academy at Varsovie.

1930. 71 A Bridal Party. Salon, '70.

BRILLOUIN (LOUIS-GEO.),
Of St. Jean d'Angely. Pupil of Drolling and Cabat.
Medals, 1865, 1869. Legion of Honor, 1870.

1000. 72 A Sermon in the Provinces, the
custom of the 18th Century.

ROSZEZEWSKI (HENRY-DOMINIQUE),
Of Chezal-Benoist.

110 73 Objects of Art.

THE MIRROR OF CATHERINE DE MEDICIS, agate
precious stones and cameos (Louvre coll.)
20

KOEK-KOEK (BAREND, CORNELIS),

Of Holland, deceased.

74 Landscape---Morning.

75   "   Evening.

PLASSAN (ANTOINE-EMILE),

Of Bordeaux. Medals, 1852, '57, '59. Legion of Honor, 1859.

76 Child with Fruit.

MEYER,

Von Bremen.

77 Vanity (oil study for picture).

ZAMACOIS (EDUARDO),

Deceased, of Bilboa, Spain. Pupil of Meissonier. Medals, 1867, '70.

78 Spanish Woman.

VIBERT (GEORGES-JEHAN),

Of Paris. Pupil of Barrias. Medals, 1864, '67, '68.

79 Spanish Matador.

21

19147.00

500

DETAILLE (JEAN-BAPTISTE),

Of Paris. Pupil of Meissonier. Medals, 1869, '70.

215 80) Lancer of Army of Napoleon I.

b. Wilmore   ...

MEYER,

Von Bremen.

130 81 The Inundation (drawing). *Edmands*

19.492.00

Second Evening's Sale

WEDNESDAY, APRIL 24.

19 49 2

60 FRERE (CHAS. THEODORE),

Of Paris. Pupil of Cogniet and Roqueplan. Medals,
1848 and '65.

135 82 Evening near Cairo. *Isane Bull 45 South*

150 ESBENS (ETIENNE-EMILE),

Of Bordeaux. Pupil of Gerome.

105 83 The Lizard. *M. H. Silling art = 5 15*

23

19. 732

19732.

BOUCHARD (PIERRE-LOUIS),
17⁵ Of Lyon. Pupil of Flandrin.

100. 84 **Brittany Girl Knitting.**
641

ROBINSON (W.),
3⁰⁰ Of London.

80 85 **The Pet Fawn.**

MOORMANS (FRANCOIS-LÉONARD),
1⁰⁰ Of Rotterdam. Pupil of the Academy of Antwerp.

105 86 **The Armorer.** *13 Lily 554*

SIMPSON, (W. P.),
21⁰ Of London.

55 87 **" Dignity and Impudence."**

(Enamel Painting, after Landseer.)

15⁰ **SAUVAGE (PHILLIPE),**
Of Villers-le-Bel. Pupil of Dupuis and Dansaert.

195 88 **" Don't Wake Sister."**
24 *Geo J. Nelson 2 £ 35*

20.26⁷

ANDERSON (W.),

Of London.

89 Santa Claus.

BOURGOIN (ADOLPHE),

Of Paris.   Pupil of Delaroche and Cogniet.

90 The New Novel.

LENOIR (PAUL-MARIE),

Of Paris.   Pupil of Gerome and Jalabert.

91 Arab Messenger.

BECKER (GEORGES),

Of Paris.   Pupil of Gerome.   Medal, 1870.

92 The Anniversary.

DE NOTER (DAVID),

Of Brussels.

93 Fruits, Flowers, &c.

25

21.137

HADAMARD (AUGUSTE),

570 Of Metz. Pupil of Delaroche.

200 94 The Reprimand. (Ex. in ·Salon, 1870.) *Bryan 361 1820*

GLAIZE (PAUL-LEONE),

Of Paris. Pupil of his father and Gerome. Medals. *500* 1864, '66, '68.

420 95 Study in a Garden.

RISSE (ROLAND),

500 Of Cologne. Pupil of Schadow.

210 96 The Prince awaking the Sleeping Beauty. *T.D. Reilly 5 113*

ANDERSON (Mrs. S.),

6 Of London.

210 97 The Puzzle in Arithmetic.

" Multiplication is vexation,
Division is as bad ;
The rule of three puzzles me,
And practice drives me mad."

22·177

ALBOY-REBOUET (ALFRED),

Of Paris. Pupil of Gleyre and Gerome.

98 Making Waffles---"Hallow Eve."

RUDAUX (EDMOND-ADOLPHE),

Of Verdun. Pupil of Boulanger and Lavielle.

99 Decision of the Flower.

SCHELFHOUT (ANDREAS),

Of the Hague, deceased.

100 Winter in Holland.

SEIGNAC (PAUL),

Of Bordeaux. Pupil of Picot and Frere.

101 Boy with Bird Cage.

DIEFFENBACH (ANTOINE),

Of Wiesbaden. Pupil of Jordan.

102 Girl and Goat.

LADDELL (C.),

5w

Of London.

14f 103 Grapes, Peaches, &c., with Tazza by Cellini. *Barker*

LEYENDECKER (PAUL),

8w

Of Paris. Pupil of Gerome.

250 104 The Casket of Jewels. *J. & Vo,.*

JOURDAN (ADOLPHE),

6w

Of Nimes. Pupil of Jalabert. Medals, 1864, '66, '69.

30f 105 He don't want to go In. *J. P. Blossom*

KAEMMERER (FREDERICH HENRI),

3w

Of the Hague. Pupil of Gerome.

130 106 Garden of Luxembourg.

COOMANS (JOSEPH),

3w

Of Brussels.

250 107 Pompeian Lady.

28

4.437

14.137 2w **LEFEVRE (ADOLPHE-RENÉ),**
Of Paris. Pupil of Tony Bergues (deceased).

115 108 The Studio of Adriaan Vander Werff. *Lr. A. Clark 237 Renal*

100 **DETAILLE (JEAN BAPTISTE),**
Of Paris. Pupil of Meissonier. Medals, 1869, '70.

350 109 A Reconnoissance---War of 1812.
G.P. Helm ne 130 5 i r

750 **DONEAUD (JEAN-EUGENE),**
Of Paris. Pupil of Flandrin.

365 110 The Triumphal Procession. Salon, '70. *J.E. Zuller B.'.*

JACOBS (FRANCOIS),
550 Of Brussels.

800 111 Interior, Lady with Parrot.
J. au ; n r 29 15 2r 36

25.267.

25.267

BRILLOUIN (LOUIS-GEORGES),

Of St. Jean d'Angely. Pupil of Drolling and Cabat.
1 5~ Medals, 1865, '69. Legion of Honor, 1870.

800 112 Siege Operations.

COROT (JEAN-BAPTISTE),

Of Paris. Pupil of V. Bertin. Medals, 1833, 1848, 1855,
1867. Legion of Honor, 1846, 1857.

315 113 Landscape, Spring.

ESBENS (ETIENNE-EMILE),

8~ Of Bordeaux. Pupil of Gerome.

310 114 Arab Soldiers. *Edwards*

MURILLO-BRACHO,

1 7 0 Of Spain. Pupil of the Academy of Arts at Malaga.

230 115 Grapes of the Province of Malaga. *J.B. Blossom*

PIOT (ANTOINE),

125~ Of Paris. Pupil of Delaroche and Galliat.

700 116 The Rose-Bud. *C.P. Huntington*
30 *65 Park Avenue*

7.622

CARAUD (JOSEPH),

Of Cluny. Pupil of Pujol and Muller. Medals, 1859, '61, '63. Legion of Honor, '67.

117 The Pet Kitten.

BOUCHARD (PIERRE-LOUIS),

Of Lyons. Pupil of Flandrin.

118 Young Italian Girl.

RUDAUX (EDMOND-ADOLPHE),

Of Verdun. Pupil of Boulanger and Laveille.

119 Smitten.

BERANGER (JEAN BAPTISTE),

Of Sevres. Pupil of Delaroche. Medals, 1846, '48.

120 In the Studio.

ESBENS (ETIENNE-EMILE),

Of Bordeaux. Pupil of Gerome.

121 Missed his Lesson.

31

PREYER (EMILIE),
Of Dusseldorf. Pupil of her father.

3 ∾

170 122 Grapes, Plums, &c. *C. a Lamont*
555. S' ar

FAUVELET (JEAN),
Of Bordeaux. Pupil of Delacour. Medal, 1848.

9 ∾

120 123 The Studio. *Bryan 361 U 20*

CASTRES (EDOUARD),
Of Geneva. Pupil of Zamacois.

5 ∾

75 124 Japanese Interior. *J. L. Rule, 11 Est*

SUS (GUSTAV),
Of Dusseldorf.

1 ∾

125 125 More free than Welcome---"Hun-
ger knows no law." *od. S, uk*
13 3 42

BOULANGER (GUSTAV-RODOLPHE),
Of Paris. Pupil of Delaroche and Jollivet. Prize of
Rome, 1849. Medals, 1857, '59, '63. Legion of
Honor, 1865.

15 ∾

325

126 Turkish Nurse and Child. *A. L. Reaver Weir*

1.677

LESREL (ADOLPHE-ALEXANDRE),

19.672 *200* Of Genets. Pupil of Gerome.

155 127 Fancy Head. *J. B. Blossom Brooklyn*
155 128   "   "

GUES (ALFRED),

800 Of Montargis. Pupil of Gleyre.

395 129 A Page Singing.

200 TOULMOUCHE (AUGUSTE),

Of Nantes. Pupil of Gleyre. Medals, 1852, '59, '61.

130 " What does it mean ?"

COOMANS (JOSEPH),

1 200 Of Brussels.

635 131 The Kiss, Pompeiian Interior.

31.012.

31.012

HÜBNER (JULIUS),

500   Of Dusseldorf. Pupil of his father.

440 132 " John Anderson my Joe." *M. in it*

BRILLOUIN (LOUIS-GEORGES),

6 w

Of St. Jean d'Angely. Pupil of Drolling and Cabat.
Medals, 1865, 1869. Legion of Honor, 1870.

330 133 The Antiquarian. *C, a Lamont*

DETAILLE (JEAN-BAPTISTE),

15 w

Of Paris. Pupil of Meissonier. Medals, 1869, '70.

500 134 The Invader --- Prussian Soldier,
        1870. *C, a Lamont*

SCHMIDT (ED. ALLAN),

Of Dusseldorf.

640 135 In the Laboratory.
            34   *J. d. 1634*

32.922

LESREL (ADOLPHE-ALEXANDRE).

Of Genets. Pupil of Gerome.

610. 136 The Beautiful Vase.

TISSOT (JAMES).

Of Nantes. Pupil of Flandrin and Lamothe. Medal. 1866.

137 German Lady of the XVth Century.

MEYER,

Von Bremen.

138 "Please help a Poor Boy."

CARAUD (JOSEPH),

Of Cluny. Pupil of Pujol and Muller. Medals, 1859, '61, '63. Legion of Honor, '67.

139 Preparing the Dessert.

36402

COMTE (PIERRE CHARLES),

Of Lyon. Pupil of R. Fleury. Medals, 1853, '55, '57, '67.
Legion of Honor, 1857.

415. 140 Going out for a Walk---Time,
Henri IV, of France.

DELAROCHE (PAUL),

Born in Paris, 1797. Died there, 1856. Pupil of Gros.

141 St. Madeline on her way to Mar-
seilles, time of the Plague.

*Study (1835) made for the Church of the Madeline, but never
painted. This study was sold with the effects of the artist,
12th June, 1857, lot No. 22 on catalogue.*

WILLEMS (FLORENT),

DE NOTER (DAVID),

Of Brussels. Medals, 1844, '46, '53, '67. Legion of Honor,
1857.

670 142 An Abundant Larder.

GIDE (THEOPHILE),

Of Paris. Pupil of Delaroche and Cogniet. Medals,
1861, '65, '66. Legion of Honor, 1866.

485 143 Sisters of Charity.

36

379; 2

VOLTZ (F.),

Of Munich.

1300 144 Cattle and Figures.

ROSZEZEWSKI (HENRY-DOMINIQUE),

500 Of Chezal Benoist.

530 145 Objects of Art.

AGATE PITCHER, with head of Minerva for cover,
enamelled by Cellini. Rock Crystal Mirror, in
miniature frame of carved wood, Flemish work
16th century. Ebony and Steel Box (Louvre
coll.) Bowl, in form of a shell, Venetian glass,
15th century. Agate Cup, with cover (Catherine de Medicis). Fan, of blue silk, with guipure
lace, Handkerchief of same, Louis 13th Turkish
Tapestry (from a private coll).

ESCOSURA (IGNACE DE LEON),

Of Spain. Pupil of Gerome. Commander of the Order
of Isabella of Spain. Chevalier of the Order of
150 Charles III, of Spain, and Chevalier of the Order of
Christ, of Portugal.

800 146 "Time is Money."

37 6 & 38

40.602

40602

BERANGER (JEAN-BAPTISTE),

Of Sevres. Pupil of Delaroche. Medals, 1846, '48.

665 147 A Rose among the Thorns.

VERBOECKHOVEN (EUGENE),

Of Brussels. Medals, 1824, '41, '45, '55. Legion of Honor, 1855, &c., &c.

465 148 Winter Scene in Holland.

ZAMACOIS (EDUARDO),

Deceased, of Bilbao, Spain. Pupil of Meissonier. Medals, 1867, '70.

735 149 The Morning Call.

VIBERT (GEORGES JEHAN),

Of Paris. Pupil of Barrias. Medals, 1864, '67, '68.

655 150 Spanish Cook---"Too Hot."

MEYER,

Von Bremen.

235 151 Evening Prayer (drawing).

38

RICHARDS (WM. T.).

Of Philadelphia.

152 Snow Squall---New Jersey Coast.

J. B. Blossom

JOHNSON (EASTMAN).

Of New York.

153 Harpers' Weekly---At Nantucket.

Harper

DE VRIENDT (ALBERT),

Of Brussels.

154 The Studio of an Image Maker---
15th Century. *J. Millbank*
6. & 38

Extract of Letter from the Artist.

The painting on the subject of which you desire some information,
I had entitled " *The Studio of Master Jehan, the Image Maker.*"
This artist, of whom the chronicles of the 15th century speaks, is
probably Jean Hossie, who painted for the Duke of Bourgogon.

As for the visitors, I did not have the intention to make these per-
sonages historical.

[Signed.] ALBERT D'VRIENDT.

39

45.472

BOUGHTON (GEO. H.),

Of Albany,

2.200 155 Colder than Snow. *I. millbank*
6 E 38

From Royal Academy, Ex. 1871.

Notice from the " Athenæum."

" A picture of Sunday Morning at a French town, about date of 1400, and called by Mr. Boughton 'Colder than Snow,' (99) represents the hopeless seeking of a lady's love by a youth

' The winter's wind is not more chill
Than the cold smile they fain would win.'

" The scene is the exterior of a castle of about the 14th century, in snowy weather. The figures traverse a draw-bridge on their way to prayer; the lady is attended by her lovers, a page follows bearing books on a cushion. This picture is well and pleasantly painted ; the frigid expression of the lady's face and the urgent look of the suitors are ably and suitably given."

" London Times."

" Mr. Boughton's picture is a middle-aged lesson to old and young gentlemen who are fools enough to fall in love with a coquette. The costumes are true, rich and graceful. The back ground of Mediæval town, which looms faintly through frost-fogged air, is capitally done."

" London Graphic"

' Mr. Boughton in this important work displays very decided improvement.''

Correspondent of " Cincinnati Commercial."

" A larger and more elaborate picture, and one from which I anticipate great celebrity, is offered this year by our Boughton, and represents a princess emerging from the castle gateway, going to her religious devotions. She is beautiful, but 'Colder than the Snow' which covers the hard, gray battlements around her, and on which she treads. On each side a courtier walks, vainly seeking to win a smile from her lovely face. * * * * In short, as an American I am proud of Boughton and of the rank he is maintaining in the Old World. That rank he has reached by patient work as well as by genius."

47.672

BOUGUEREAU (WILLIAM-ADOLPHE),

Of La Rochelle. Pupil of Picot. Prize of Rome, 1850. Medals, 1855, '57, '59, '63. Universal Exhibition of 1867. Legion of Honor, 1859.

156 The Canephoros.

Extract of Letter from the Artist.

LA ROCHELLE, 1871.

Mr. AVERY:—The large picture which you recently bought of me, and for which you have sent me the sum total in payment, through Mr. ——, represents the Canephoros, young Greeks of old, going to a sacrifice, for which they carry different utensils.*

In this picture I have sought to make, above all, a beautiful study of man, without, however, neglecting the women. And you must think that I have succeeded since you have bought it of me. This is a great satisfaction to me.

[Signed.]   WM. BOUGUEREAU.

* When a sacrifice was to be offered, the round cake, the chaplet of flowers, or leaves, the knife used to slay the victim and sometimes the frank-incense, were deposited in flat circular baskets, and this was frequently carried by a virgin on her head to the altar. The practice was observed more especially at Athens, when a private man sacrificed, either his daughter, or some unmarried female of his family, officiated as his Canephoros ; but in the Panathénaea, the Dionysia and other public festivals, two virgins of the first Athenian families were appointed for the purpose. Their function is described by Ovid.

www.ingramcontent.com/pod-product-compliance
Lightning Source LLC
Chambersburg PA
CBHW021550270326
41930CB00008B/1440